ONE MAN'S JOURNEY

One Man's Journey.

Books may be purchased in quantity and/or special sales
by contacting the author, Reginald Thomas at
www.reginaldthomasbooks.com.

Requests for speaking engagements may be submitted at
www.reginaldthomasbooks.com

ISBN: 9798633171563

Design by www.thedesignbrand.com

CONTENTS

INTRODUCTION

Being confident of this very thing, that he which hath begun a good work in you will perform it until the day of Jesus Christ.

Philippians 1:6

Any driver can tell you that a trip can be hindered by several things. Weather, accidents, and construction just to name a few. The ultimate goal is to reach a predetermined destination. The same can be said of the journey called life. In this expedition we are often hindered by bills, health issues, and family crisis. Yet the mission is the same. The predetermined destination called destiny. No one likes getting lost and asking for directions is a bit uncomfortable. Perhaps you have found yourself off course. Things haven't gone quite the way you had hoped. Dreams once on the forefront of your mind have started to fade away. Just as we are determined to reach that appointment, lunch date, or getting the kids, our focus should be firmly fixed, divinely directed by GPS. What has been determined, destined, and purposed has to be. God is not a man, that he should lie, nor a son of man, that he should repent hath he said, and shall he not do it? Or hath he spoken, and shall he not make it good? (Numbers 23:19).

ADULLAM

Never thought I'd be in this place
Can we take the good and not the bad?
Steps of peace have left no trace
Days spent recounting what I once had

Tried every way to express how I feel
Should I even try
Guess I'm stuck with this raw deal
Left alone and wondering why

CIVIL

Societal norms are that one should be polite
To me this notion is so contrite

Gentile and kind, one must be politically correct
Causes most to keep what's real in check

The veil of the heart most often a smile
Truth be told, you're off by a mile

Reality truth what's really inside
I'm a fake the truth I can no longer hide

Bitterness anger and rage are my pillow at night
Passion is my biggest fight

To be held loved touched and kissed,
Things I want and truly miss

My frame is to be quaint
The lies make me want to faint

O how I want to be free
O how I want to be me

COOL

I've tried my best to be cool
This drool from my face like a fool

Trying is not the concern
The real me, what do you discern?

Everybody has a mark
Noah was destined to build the ark

That thing you were destined to make
Cooking is a gift what do you want to bake

Stop trying to be cool
What you are is not stupid and cruel

We are different for a reason
Embrace this, your season

Unique and wonderful you are
He sees you from afar

COLOR BLIND

Why do you insist on judging me?
Without knowing anything about what you see

My skin is darker
Get to know me; try a little harder

Why throw darts
Do you know what's in my heart?

Keep your cold shoulder
My deeds must be much bolder

Those who know me know that I love babies
Sweet little faces drive me crazy

Admiring how they are mine
Dreaming they grow up color blind

CREW

Where did you go? think I'll take a look
You said we got you, can't let you off the hook

Till the end we will be
Let us wait and see

When you're needed the most, you can't be found
Looked everywhere all-around town

He's a mess; what did you do
Maybe it was his new boo

Besides this trouble, the worst thing is being alone
Put a fork in him he's done

CRYSTAL BALL

Mankind has an undying need to know what lies
ahead
Wanting to know when and how of fears to dread

Searching for clues that will determine a mate
Fear of the unknown is the key of fate

Maybe endless hours spent at the local bar
Sheer ignorance may leave one with scars

Looking for answers may lead one to some strange
places
The choices and decisions may look like an
overwhelming oasis

You ask friends and may read a book in hope of
advice
Many things you ponder may surface even twice

Too bad I had to take this fall
Didn't have a crystal ball

Answers were concealed by an unfamiliar face
A mighty gift we recognize as grace

DAISIES

They stand with their heads up high
Glory and honor that would reach the sky

Hate and disgrace are things they don't show
The stories they could tell only heaven knows

What amazes me the most is their lack of fear
They do not panic nor ever shed a tear

For soon they know time comes to an end
No cries of despair or guilt to defend

The life she is given is lived to its best
Soon her soul will be at rest

Why my friend do we live life with no regard
Taking chances in life, the shuffle of cards

All night we sit by the bed
Memories of time gone by, dances in our heads

Stuff long done; wow how crazy!
Wish I was more like daisies

DECREE

A bright beginning is now an end
My sight now on the mend

Great you shall be
A farce, that crazy decree

A king now lost in the cold
Anointed, you were told

O how you should keep your lies
Prayers gone lost in the skies

Hope deferred makes one sick
Absolute faith gone so quick

DESTINY

Where was I before my birth
Where will I be after my death

This thing we call life and time

When did it start?
When will it end?

Life can deal several hands

To some joy and peace
Others pain and despair

Why are some people

Smart, educated and full of dreams
Others poor, isolated, and hopeless it seems

How much of our lives do we control?

Is it simply destiny?

DIRECTION

To thee, my soon coming King
To you the plea of my soul does ring

Love and kindness, you have never withheld
In your presence I want to dwell

Show me what you see
Sweet savior when thine eyes see me

No atlas or map can save me now
My way back to you, oh show me how

Thine light shine so bright
To save me oh, so contrite

ELECTION YEAR

If you have not heard it's another election year
Politicians are our friends; we have nothing to fear

Read your newspaper and watch the news
If you are not careful, you will catch the blues

Promises they never keep,
Gentle as sheep

Jeremiah was told to see one that strives for justice
and truth
They acted as if these things were like a bad tooth

He found out they had no idea of which way to go
He even went to the rich and they did not know

It is another election year
Yes, we have much to fear

FALL

It wasn't a hill or a mountain
Nor a slip of drips from a fountain

No height was the beginning of this trouble
A bully didn't defeat me in a rumble

Integrity and luck, was the start of my descent
My own heart do I hate and resent

Lies and morality are not my companions
My crown now lies in a canyon

FORFEIT

Now this is the reason
To everything there is a season

Some to live and some to die
The real reason I will not lie

I'm done, that's it
Yep, I quit

You win. Game over
Leave me alone. Go be with your lover

To you is the greatest prize
Go ahead; send your spies

It's over. I have no more breath
Now is my destiny with death

FREEDOM

A king once stood and told of his dream

An inheritance of this great nation

Could it be that it was just a scheme

Or a bold attempt to bring justification

First began with a king on a cross

To make right the cost of sin

Once bound for eternity and my soul lost

Freedom now and for eternity as it should have been

FRIENDSHIP

True friendship is precious and rare

Its treasure is not composed of diamonds or rubies

It contains love that is unconditional and sincere

Friendship will not sit by and see you starve

Out of her own mouth she will give you the last piece

When no one else will listen, she does to every word

You do not bare your burdens alone

On her shoulder she claims as her own

Separation does not mean you are alone

Because of friendship she will always have your heart

Thanks for being a friend

GOOD GUYS

Dear brother,

Let not your heart be troubled

The pain in your heart is evident in every move you make

There is only one true question:

Why is it, good guys never win?

We are mistreated and misunderstood

People take our strength as a weakness

Many times, our hearts are trampled on like a dirty rag

Instead of being called by our true names

Dear brother,

Let not your heart be troubled

Live as a true man should

It is written the meek shall inherit the earth

Let not your heart be troubled

We shall have the last laugh

HERO

You do not have blazing speed
But sincere acts are your deeds

No one sees you leaping huge mountains
Maybe lifting a kid up to a fountain

Your treasures are not stored in a bank
Nor do we find you trying to pull rank

Small arms that can't lift a car
Trying his best, you won't find him in a bar

Girls do not come and flock to his shoulder
In his deeds to mankind, he must be much bolder

He does not seek fortune or fame
Because one day those things go up in flames

You will not find him near a crowd
In the end he will float above the clouds

My hero is no ordinary man
Do not fret, you do have fans

HOPE

You have deceived me too long
You liar, your stories are all wrong

Images of the future you have painted
Trouble and headache, you are now tainted

A wedding and honeymoon will be soon
Dreams have drifted further than the moon

I want to despise you but I dare,
One day save me from my despair

INNOCENCE

No sir you're not off the hook,
Look at what you really took

Dreams and innocence lost
Trying to show me that you're the boss

How dare you hide now
You coward and this is how

Stealing a boy
Like he was a toy

Wished you stayed from where you came
This monster I cannot contain

JOCKS

Tough, and you get the girls
Many are like you all around the world

On my tv and pc
The annual trip you make to DC

Rich and famous your talents have made you
To gifts you are certainly true

My attempts have failed
Trips to the gym--I have bailed

Forgive me of my envy
Certainly, you are not my enemy

We all have a path
Finding mine is my task

LAMENTATIONS

From the darkest place of my existence
Do you reside and have no resistance?

Loud and bold you make your plea
Everyone can hear and clearly see

No shame in telling the truth
You have shaken me, even my tooth

Can't hide or refrain from making your decree
To live or move forward, I do concede

No strength or might are results of my sin
Not from an enemy, just what's within

KITCHEN

To the kitchen we would sit
Chatting about life a bit

This summit was not of dishes
A mother telling her son of dreams she wishes

A future most bright
Could not be obtained without a fight

The choice of beverage is coffee in a mug
The reins of my heart she would tug

LION

King of the jungle and mighty you are
Your roar can be heard from miles afar

Strength and power, that's your game
Rise against him and leave the fight lame

You rule and all others know
Thine splendor is yours and we bow below

No one questions the reign of your throne
Any rebellion you fool and you will be done

Yes, does my futile heart shake
Guess I thought it was me, now I'm awake

MAGIC

The allusion is to make something disappear
Laughter, applause, most often a joke
To be gone, to be lost is the fear
This pain is what I want to revoke
No schemes or tricks to hide the things that are near
Cries are ignored and never heard
Happens to many but to me, an illusion
To be free of shackles, a dream most absorbed
No magic for me is the conclusion

MOVIES

Coming to America was my first big show
Watching this king caused my face to glow

Hundreds now in the index
A moment now to reflect

You are my escape from reality
Filled with missteps and brutality

Some make me laugh and cry
Makes me sad when the hero dies

You are my hiding place indeed
The fight for my life I do concede

MR. PRESIDENT

Your job is one that has serious implications
One mistake and we could face another holocaust
Decision after decision, do you ever get any sleep
Only four years and so much to do
This morning as you looked out your window
What did you see?
Men and women at your command
Another decision you must make
When you sit with your cabinet weighing the odds
Mr. President please consider this unheard song
When you sat down at your seat
Someone did not have bread for their kid
The secret service protects you and your family
Our families face death in drugs and disorder
The line of defense is weary worn faith
A father tells his kids we have no money

TICKET

You are special, unique indeed
Only you can provide a special need

Entrance you give to many events
Movies, parks, and three big tents

Escape you give to most,
A pleasant and honorable host

Mine has been denied
No truth, to me you lied

Freedom, joy, and peace
What I really want is a release

VERDICT

Murder was not the weapon of choice
A knife was not the reason for this mess
This situation is no reason to rejoice
Could it be this is a test?

Every action has a reaction
Sentences have reason
Slipping so hard I have no traction
Time should have been subtracted

A long look has caused me to think
What happened? I was just in the kitchen
It happened so fast I didn't even blink,
The reason why is I didn't listen

WHAT DO YOU SEE?

What do you see?

When you look into the eyes of a child

A mold of clay without ignorance and hate

With the proper love, guidance, and education

Can be transformed into anything you can imagine

What do you see?

When you look into the eyes of a child

The perfect idealism of human nature

That all of mankind should seek

A life, that for now is immaculate, naïve, spotless, and pure

What do you see?

When you look into the eyes of a child

WINDOW

Your task is to be open
To show what doesn't have to be spoken

One reality seen from two sides
Which is correct, how do you decide?

You can see a gent tying his tie
What is he doing? Maybe hiding his lies

What is he trying to hide?
The reality of what's inside

Lost, angry, and sad
Things he did makes him mad

Hiding his shame
Is now his game

DECEIT

We're at war with an enemy that's complex

His goal is to seek and destroy

You can find your life in a mess

No instruction on how to protect yourself

Finally, he reveals himself

His weapons are treacherous lies

Understanding him can be a little slippery

Painting a picture of beauty and grace

Its existence will leave you a disgrace

Promises to take you to a special place

Facing this enemy is now a test

Try hard to do your best

You have been given your direction

No introduction is needed

Maybe now

Maybe later

One night as you fall asleep

Could be hanging with a friend

Please be careful

Someday we all face deceit

DEATH

We all have been to that familiar place
You identify a familiar face

As someone lowers them into the ground
A broken heart continually pounds

Death has been stated as being without life
Why is your heart full of strife?

You go home and pick up the pieces
Wondering what makes us superior species

Death has been stated as being without
What is that all about

Is it possible to be alive in a physical sense?
Dead in the heart is what you really resent

Your hands are open wide in need of love
What you receive is a hard-felt shove

Please listen. Will you sit and talk?
In denial? Let's go for a walk

Trying hard for some quality time
That ain't worth a dime

So, you say death is a state of being without
Deep in my being, I know something about

Hours spent all alone
Waiting for someone to pick up the phone

No, you can't find me in a casket
A life torn and a little retched

My death is a state of being without
Who I am leaves me in doubt

DREAMS

Direct interpretation of the soul

Not even real, no concrete

Representing your deepest secrets

Some may be of joy and happiness

Tasting her lips

Coming off the bench to save the day

Holding your baby for the first time

Dreading when they say, "can I go out?"

Some a business and empire

A romantic and tranquil place

We all have them

What's your dream?

EMPTY

To most a familiar scenario,

Surrounded by people and things

Family, school, and friends

Time passes and something changes

We are consumed by a different animal

Time now wedged between decisions and dates

Maybe I'll give it some time

Alarmed both day and night

Unlike you, my life is different

Beneath the hustle and bustle

In the depth of a soul

Now a man and all that jazz

My days are filled with stuff

Yet I am empty

A piece of the puzzle is still missing

Long days and even nights

A void that hasn't been fulfilled

HOW MANY MILES

How many miles must one travel?

In search of a special place

It could be near but so very far

How many miles must one travel?

Walking to find that you are lost

Once dreams were clear and near

Now you wonder like a man in space

Thrown by spite and shame,

This place I long for is all so sweet

A map or compass are not needed

For the path was very clear

My destiny, future, and fate

Decisions made and choices chosen

My physical state is clearly known

My heart is the one lost

How many miles must I travel?

To hear son, you are forgiven

LIFE

Concealed and limited to the naked eye,
Men tremble trying to answer the question why

Scholar seeking a reasonable resolution
To a journey, a time yours and mine, what's the
solution

Doves fly with beauty and grace
Take your time, a journey and not a race

To each his own time
Yes, yours and mine

To define, some spin the dice
Trying to find the meaning of life

LIES

Some are large or small
Embrace one and take a fall

Leaving in its path destruction
Life now needing reconstruction

Repaired from being torn down
No need to go downtown

Could be, you didn't know
You put on a good show

Someone only wanted a peak
Your crazy freak

You say no food, no money
But you gave it to your honey

You said it's you that makes my life complete
Fooled me in your nice retreat

Inside I want to die
Found out, we were a lie

LISTEN TO YOUR HEART

A situation that you don't know what to do
Wanting to talk, but to who?

Parents listen but do they understand
Time passes by like the number of sands

Fear shown by your tears
Decisions leave you in constant fear

For the rest of my life
Not wanting to live in strife

Before us a judgement day
We all have a price to pay

Ask a friend he gives you a book
Did you know he was a crook?

Considering her to be his wife
Got stabbed in the back, didn't see the knife

A proposal for marriage
Let's drive off in this beautiful carriage

Fears and ignorance found in abuse
Ashamed of your business leaves you a recluse

Every day we face decisions
Prayers prayed with precision

Most of us simply don't know what to do
Searching for someone to talk to, who?

For every decision, a price to pay
Right or wrong it won't go away

LOOK INSIDE

Your search is endless and has no boundaries

Looking for a reason for your living

To the depths of hell, you gladly go

The heights of heaven are no real challenge

The reward is your very soul

Space and time are irrational

They don't exist in space and time

Without sleep or food

A man on a mission

Searching for what he really wanted

Consider this notation

Let the search led you inside

To the heart he always speaks

FREE

You exist in the truest realm of humanity
Only to be ridiculed and misunderstood
Not often someone calls you their own
The fruits of thine labor is peace and tranquility
Fools rather have turmoil and disgrace
Secrets kept in the dark
Truth I'm told, sets you free

MAD

It happened. I don't understand
Situations that can't be explained
Things to do and so little time
Questions and no answers
My head hurts and my mouth is dry
Go quickly my friend
A little irate and irrational
If you must know
I'm mad

MASKS

Behind your smile I see a frown

Thoughts of happiness-- are you really sad?

Trying to turn madness into joy

Praying to heaven don't want to go to hell

Encouraging words to lift you up

Still feeling a little down

Deceived, you have been unmasked

MERCY

My soul cries and you can't see the tears

They are hidden from the naked eye and fall

What has happened to me?

That befalls inhumane cruelty

My being has been forsaken and withdrawn from me

You have wavered any concern for me

Left with no hope or sense of direction

Hear my plea

Have mercy on me

MISTAKES

From conception till death, we all have decisions
Educated or illiterate
Your financial status, who cares?
No regard to your physical state
From conception till death, we all have decisions
They all should be given special consideration
If answers are unknown, seek wholesome advice
Prayers should be the first line of defense
Listen to instruction
From conception till death, we all have decisions
Please listen and pay close attention
Choices are chosen without intervention
Let faith be your right-hand man
From conception till death, we all have decisions
Pray for direction
Make one wrong choice
It could be that one big mistake
From conception till death, we all have decisions

MIRRORS

Mirrors are an interesting device
Your only job is to give a reflection
Too bad you can't see my heart full of strife
Tried to hide it with medication

The truth-- we don't want to see
What some would call reality
Hurt so bad, why me
Trying to escape this brutality

NIGHTMARE

In this dream was a great descent
My own life, I'd began to resent

A pit was now my home
Falling, without no love to be shone

Grander and purpose were lost
The price of neglect was the cost

Hope abandoned,
Without understanding

My dream, now a nightmare
Awake, I can only stare

OBEDIENCE

We have a duty that is often ignored,

Given little thought or much regard

For every situation, an answer

Tucked away in the good book

Seek him, and your days will be many

Your enemies will become your footstool

A path now made very clear

Dig a ditch for you and to them it will be

Tears caught by the creator himself

Listen to instruction and give heed to wisdom

Pray nonstop and please read

Told to seek him and righteousness

To avoid the pitfalls of life

Obey him only and early if you must

ON YOUR OWN

For one day my son, you will be on your own
Dust I will be, but my heart have you known

Instruction and wisdom son, do you understand
Please listen to this and not the band

For one day my son, you will be on your own
Take full advantage of what you have been shown

QUARANTINED

Loathed and despised,
Humor you refuse to do
They have tried and failed to reprise
Like an animal caged in a zoo

No sunset to rest my weary soul,
This pit is now my home
Contained, because I'm a troll
Paraded and mocked like a gnome,

Hugs and kisses have been refused
Passion and peace have lost its lease
Why me, the question that leaves me confused
Got me locked up like you're the police

REMORSE

Often in life, we face a cruel monster

He is seeking someone to conquer

His arrival is often and without warning

Even in the midst of friends

Some while lying in bed

He doesn't want your flesh

What's desired is your soul

You can be fooled--he takes many shapes

True love lost,

Maybe a misunderstanding

His daggers are hurt, pain, and regret

He can be called many things,

Let's call him regret

RENEW MY STRENGTH

Here I am waiting in a hospital bed
Many thoughts are going through my head

Will God allow me to wake up?
Maybe it's time to give up

The verdict was a lifetime of pain
Is there anything left for me to gain

Football was my dream I gave up a quitter
That experience left me bitter

We realize that there is hope
It didn't come from dope

In a very special place,
My hands upon my face

In his presence is the fullness of joy
Renewing a scared man, really a boy

SEARCH

You and I we may be different
Clearly, we are not the same
Crazy how we share the same resentment,
Trying hard to hide the shame

Looking anywhere, a deep search
Did terrible things to hide the pain
Didn't find it on the perch
Finding you is something to gain

Acceptance, purpose, and peace
Searching near and far
Hiding behind this ugly fleece
Can you see my scar?

TRAPPED

Freedom is a state of mind
You think you see, but you're blind

The heart is constrained
Pain, he cannot contain

Not in a cage or a cell
Wish you knew my face doesn't tell

Held by fears,
Can't see my tears

I want to be free
Can't you see?

No, you can't
The past, I can't recant

DESSERT

You are my favorite part of the meal
Soft and sweet,
Tender and moist
Some are small and that's ok
Others large, now that's even better
What you add to the meal is unique
It was sent straight from the heavens
I have worked hard all day
It's time to go home
A piece of desert is all that's on my mind
The meal is cooked and everything is ready
Honey let's skip dinner
I really want some dessert

GRAPES

Grapes are perhaps my favorite fruit

Tasty and sweet, pure ecstasy

Different tones, shapes, and sizes

I love them all just the same

Can't eat just one

I'd prefer two, one in each hand

Some are small, then some large

Grapes are perhaps my favorite fruit

Conflicting measurements they have

Nice and round not hard but sweet

Home from work and time to relax

All day thinking, I'd really like some grapes

Grapes are perhaps my favorite fruit

FOR YOU MY LOVE

Her beauty is pure, radiant, and immaculate

Your love can be overpowering and undiluted, can it ever be wrong?

The first day you came into my life, can loneliness be described as miraculous?

My mind is filled with joy as I imagine you approach your throne

Each day as my eyes open to see you is like a dream

You approach me with warm open hands

Together we make a splendid team

Our love is deeper than the beach has sand

Your eyes are more beautiful than stars against the moonlight night

Smooth and gentle is your kiss

I will fight for you with endless might

When I'm with you is a time of complete and total bliss

For me you were sent on a cloud from above

It is real or does love grow each and every day

My decree to you is all my love

What more can a man say

HUSBAND

To describe him is almost impossible
He can be different things to many people
Judging this person can be a difficult task
Some may say that he is a good friend
To others a powerful and mighty foe
Working hard all day because he is a provider
Always keeping watch as a protector should
How wonderful to feel his touch
With his gentle heart knows when to listen
To describe him is almost impossible
He can be different things to many people
So happy to say he is my husband

SOCKS

For you my dear my heart bled this song
My heart aches as your mate sits here alone

We were created for each other
Since you are gone, there will never be another

Your qualities are many, but the greatest was your love
For me you were created and sent from above

You were many things-- you are the ultimate mate
With you did I share my first date

Without you my heart is broken, lonely, and lost
To have you back I'd give anything, no matter the cost

You were my fate
In you, was no sign of hate

Nowhere to go now, my life is a blunder
Where did you go is what I now ponder

Will you come back
Put my life on track

For you my dear, my heart bleeds this song
My heart aches as your mate sits here alone

DAUGHTER

Just because she is mine
Is that a crime?

Just sitting here, I want to cry
Give me some time and you will know why

This is not an ordinary baby
Soon to grow up and be a unique lady

Get up and find her toys
Soon and you will be fighting off boys

Being worthy of her is something I am not
Thoughts of her growing up puts my stomach in
knots

We could spend hours talking at a time
Must be quality or it isn't worth a dime

This love can't be contained,
Neither can I explain

WHAT'S MY DREAM?

A good friend once asked for in the middle of the night
When there is no one else in sight

What was the one thing that caught my imagination?
There is no consolation

Anything he asked,
To make his decision would be a great task

For would it be for a noble reason
Not sincere it would last only for a season

The one that was chosen is all too real
Most of us want to know how it feels

My choice, true love,
The kind sent from above

Millions of women and you are my mate
Thankful to you for you were chosen by fate

She would rather suffer than see me unhappy,

Love and respect, most of all I am happy

A good friend once asked for in the middle of the
night
When there is no one else in sight

What was the one thing that caught my
imagination?
There is no consolation

My choice, true love,
The kind sent from above

FIRST BORN

For days at a time I'd just sit and wonder
Many things did my heart just ponder

What would she be like?
Daddy's gonna buy you a bike

What would she grow up to be?
So many things for her to see

Hope she will be really smart
Maybe she can out run a dart

Hours after hours, would we just talk?
Today let's go for a walk

Without any doubt she is a special baby,
One day a special lady

SECOND CHANCE

What a surprise, my sweet number two
Another baby what should I do?

The answer was simple and right in my face
Your sweet smile, full of grace

Gifts are many and take many forms
You are not average, nor the norm

Your beauty changes day to day
Let me brag if I may

Talented and full of style,
A shine that can be seen for miles

Forgive my crazy, I love you so much
This old man's heart, you have truly touched

SON-IN-LAW

She is yours now to keep,
Her love for you is real and deep

No longer can this father hide
His deep pride

You were not on my radar
I was looking deep and far

Who will be the one to steal her heart?
It was you from the start

Who could truly love my first born?
Peace you give me, and not a heart torn

MARY

For this occasion, you asked for one simple request
Therefore, let me do my best

No paintings to call my own
Nothing can repay the love you have shown

You would go out in the coldest night
For us and put up the biggest fight

Only a mom can appreciate the differences in us
No matter what, you never put up a fuss

Your life ain't been sweet as a rose,
Loving your children is the path you chose

We all have unspoken dreams
We could see your silent screams

From you I draw much courage,
Your voice keeps me from being discouraged

When trouble arises and your heart is full of strife
Dear mother, do not give up on life

For this occasion, you asked for one simple request
Therefore, let me do my best

PUMPKIN

Each time I see her she is more
Beautiful than the day before

If I hold her a million times
Loving her is not a crime

When she smiles, it could light
Up the darkest night

What to call her, can I think of something
Got it! you will be Pumpkin

GRANDSON

O my, how have you grown
A new love to me you have shown

Like no other is yours so true
Sweet love that comes from you

You have truly blessed us all
Your presence is not all very small

A test you have been to me,
Will I be bound or truly free?

To accept and experience something new,
A new item in my life anew

Tired I have to express
Left me in a total mess

You see no color, just real love
The kind that comes from above

Me trying to describe what you are,
Grandson you're a star!

You have shown a love I never knew,
Your kisses sweet like the morning dew

BIG BRO

O how I wanted to be like him
Big Bro--strong and wise
No flaws, my eyes were dim
To be like him, a plan no one could devise

Older, taller, he was a man
Little brother thought he was a dream
To be like him is my plan
Does he know what he truly means?

CUPCAKE

Short and stout

Short and stout

I'm a little cupcake

Short and stout

MINE

The missing piece, you make me complete
This place you have, no one can compete

How could you know
You see me through and through

Family you said, can we be
From the beginning, you were to me

Listen dear son to all I have said
Tears you have made me shed

Not of pain but of true joy
Weakness, your love has destroyed

DAYLIGHT

In the darkness shall you hide
I've looked everywhere, even outside

Can you shed your warm embrace?
Cover me with your grace

Reveal yourself so I can see
What you intended me to be

I DO

We stand and utter these words
Happiness, I can't control

Bliss will give way to reality unknown
What we do is go to his throne

I do is a commitment
I do with no resentment

CHOSEN

Born in 1969,
A life new to shine

To all is a season in time
This day is called to be mine

You will show the way
Yes, is what I say

100TH FLOOR

Up high in the midnight sky
I can't dance, but I want to try

You and I, together at last
Slow down you're going to fast

On the dance floor with you in my arms
Let me grace you with my charm

FATHER

Parts of me wanted to die
Give up, don't even try

Your word is true and I believe
You knew me when I was conceived

Purpose gives me new life
I fight on without a knife

I am told to be a good soldier
I'm tired of this weight; it's like a boulder

Father I believe in your plan for me
I'll hold on to see what it will be

Made in USA - North Chelmsford, MA

11.03.2020 1337